Europe's Welfare Burden

Europe's Welfare Burden:
The Case for Reform

Benny Carlson
Alan Deacon
Hans Hoogervorst
Wilfried Prewo
Jason A. Turner

Civitas: Institute for the Study of Civil Society
London

First published June 2002
Civitas
The Mezzanine, Elizabeth House
39 York Road, London SE1 7NQ
email: books@civitas.org.uk

ISBN 1-903 386-21 7

Typeset by Civitas
in New Century Schoolbook

Printed in Great Britain by
Hartington Fine Arts Ltd
Lancing, Sussex

Contents

Authors

Benny Carlson is associate professor of economic history at Lund University and a former journalist. His research was initially devoted to the history of economic ideas, resulting in two books, *The State as a Monster* (1994) and *The Spread of Institutionalist Ideas* (1995, in Swedish). More recently he has dealt with the problem of immigrants in Sweden's big cities. Growing interest in US ideas on the one hand and welfare and labour market problems on the other has recently resulted in two further books published by Timbro, *Welfare the American Way* (2000) and *From Welfare to Work in Michigan and Wisconsin* (2001) (both in Swedish).

Alan Deacon is professor of social policy and a member of the ESRC Research Group on Care, Values and the Future of Welfare at the University of Leeds. He is the current chair of the UK Social Policy Association, and is a former editor of the *Journal of Social Policy*. His current research interests are in the debates about the future direction of welfare reform in Britain and the US and assumptions about human nature and moral agency. His latest book *Perspectives on Welfare: Ideas, Ideologies and Policy Debates* is published by Open University Press. Lawrence Mead, a central figure in US welfare reform, has commented: 'Of the several discussions of the American poverty theorists I have read, this is easily the best'.

Hans Hoogervorst has been State Secretary for Social Affairs and Employment in the Netherlands since 1998. From 1988 to 1994 he was a policy assistant to the People's Party for Freedom and Democracy (VVD) group in the Lower House of the States General, and from 1994 to 1998 a member of the House. In the House, Mr Hoogervorst was the financial spokesman for the VVD. Previously, he worked for the National Bank in Washington DC and as policy officer for the Dutch Ministry of Finance. Mr Hoogervorst has also been chairman of the 'Stabij' organisation, which provides support for new entrepreneurs in the Hague, a member of the temporary committee supervising the Insurance Board and a member of the board of the Johns Hopkins Bologna Center.

Wilfried Prewo is Chief Executive of the Hannover Chamber of Industry & Commerce. He writes and speaks frequently on economic and social policy. In particular, he has promoted a privatisation plan for the German pension and health insurance systems and a revenue-neutral flat tax of 20 per cent for Germany. Dr Prewo holds a BA from Grinnell College and an MA and PhD from Johns Hopkins University. Prior to assuming his current position, he worked in the private sector as well as, earlier in his career, at the Kiel Institute of World Economics and the University of Texas at Austin. Dr Prewo is a fellow and board member of the Centre for the New Europe and is also active in the Christian Democratic Union.

Jason A. Turner has recently stepped down as Commissioner of Human Resources Administration for New York City. He previously served as executive director of the Center for Self-Sufficiency in Milwaukee. Mr Turner came to national prominence in the USA as the director of the Welfare Replacement Project in the state of Wisconsin. He was instrumental in the creation of 'Wisconsin Works' or 'W-2'. Before that, Mr Turner had a distinguished career in the administration of President George Bush, where he was director of the Office of Family Assistance. From 1981-1985, under President Reagan, Mr Turner was special assistant, Community Planning Development in the Department of Housing and Urban Development.

Foreword

There could be no more fitting subject for the latest in the Stockholm Network's series of publications than that of welfare reform. As its name suggests, the Network was founded on the belief that the days of the Swedish-style welfare model are numbered and that it is time for society to explore new ways of supporting citizens in times of crisis.

The term 'welfare state' has such a pleasing sound that it has become a bit like motherhood and apple pie—who on earth could be opposed to the idea of the state providing help for the sick, elderly, disabled and unemployed? Yet, commentators from all points of the political spectrum now argue that the welfare state may actually be doing the unemployed more harm than good by trapping them in a cycle of dependency, sometimes for generations.

Whether it is called 'workfare' as in America or 'making work pay' as Britain's Chancellor Gordon Brown has described it, welfare reformers agree on a fundamental point: work must be made a more attractive option than welfare. Indeed, welfare should not really be regarded as an 'option' at all but instead, as it was originally intended to be, a last resort.

It is not only welfare recipients who would benefit from reducing dependency. A life on welfare often breeds ill health, family breakdown and a host of other problems. Governments too have been hamstrung for years by their own dependency on the tax revenues required to fund ever-increasing social security commitments. This burden leaves them with less flexibility to address other, competing priorities which may be just as fundamental to the good of society. Indeed, Europe's welfare policies are far from well—they now require serious surgery.

In parts of America, as Jason Turner explains in his essay, reformers have made fundamental shifts in thinking which are now beginning to shape the way both US and European policymakers approach welfare. Importantly, they have understood that there is a huge psychological difference between just being handed money and actually being expected to meet certain obligations in return for that income.

Work is not just a means of earning a wage but is tied up with a whole range of emotions and motivations. A person on welfare could receive exactly the same amount of money for doing nothing—except turning up to collect it—as he or she could from taking a private or subsidised job. However, the value of that income is qualitatively different when the person has worked for it. Work brings self-esteem, confidence, social skills and above all the ability to get and keep more work. If we can bring people who may have spent years living on benefits out of that mindset into a world where income is again connected with work, we may have a chance of helping them to become self-sufficient and to reconnect with society.

As Alan Deacon demonstrates in his essay setting out the moral arguments for welfare reform, most welfare reformers have long been concerned with trying to pinpoint and analyse the motivations of welfare recipients. But more recently, reformers have grasped a new concept. Welfare recipients are as rational as anyone else: it is the failure of the system set up to help them, rather than of the recipients themselves, that it makes more sense to stay on welfare than to take a poorly-paid job. As Charles Murray puts it in *Losing Ground*: 'poor and non-poor alike use the same general calculus in arriving at decisions; only the exigencies are different. Poor people play with fewer chips and cannot wait as long for results. Therefore they tend to reach decisions that a more affluent person would not reach' (p.16).

These new principles, along with important practical reforms such as privatising the delivery of employment and training services, are now beginning to be applied across Europe. The timing could not be better since, as the Dutch Social Security Minister Hans Hoogervorst argues, 'there is no reason for a self-indulgent attitude in Europe' (p. 24). America is more prosperous and has better living standards than the EU. Much of this prosperity can be explained by higher labour market participation and longer hours, but the United States also has higher productivity and—crucially—a more flexible labour market than we have in Europe.

If we are to address the combined pressures of immigration, an ageing population and the continent's unfunded pension liabilities, the welfare state cannot continue in its current form. High employment rates and low taxes will be the key to ensuring Europe's competitiveness in the global economy.

Germany is at the forefront of developing this new approach to welfare reform in Europe. Politicians in the state of Hesse are piloting a Wisconsin-style approach, realising that, as Wilfried Prewo concludes in his chapter: 'citizens view welfare no longer as a burden which they have to accept in the name of solidarity, but as utterly wasteful' (pp. 43-4). In Sweden too, despite its historical preference for substantial welfare payments, some municipalities are beginning to be inspired by Danish experiments in welfare, many of which owe a large debt to the Wisconsin experience.

The rest of Europe cannot afford to rest on its laurels either. Globalisation has, as Wilfried Prewo points out, 'exposed the Achilles' heel of the welfare state' (p. 41). Now it is time to patch that wound and steer the EU back on the road to prosperity.

Helen Disney

Radical Changes to the Welfare System in the US State of Wisconsin: the Results

Jason A. Turner

Introduction

The welfare system in the US has been an institution abhorred by society because it separates the receipt of income from the need to work. But why, we might ask, do we think of work as so necessary to legitimise income?

> '*In order for welfare's corrosive effect to end, work and income must once again be inseparably joined.*'

In the US, with its tradition of self-reliance, full membership in society anticipates contributions to the whole through work, and able-bodied adults who choose not to work are often perceived by Americans as lacking full social membership. Moreover work, by offering individuals the opportunity to serve others by producing valuable goods and services, fulfils a basic human need which exists beyond a particular culture. In order for welfare's corrosive effect to end, work and income must once again be inseparably joined.

Because welfare in the US is not seen as an acceptable alternative to self-reliance through employment, many national reform attempts were made in the three decades between 1960 and 1990. These reforms, passed by the Congress and each heralded at the time, resulted in no fundamental changes to the core element of welfare as an entitlement to income based on one's low-income status alone.

One former governor of California, Ronald Reagan, attempted to introduce work programmes for those receiving benefits within his state during the 1960s. But these attempts, though popular with the voters, were met with substantial resistance by the legislature and subtle resistance by the welfare government bureaucracies, and the resulting reforms were modest in scale.

The political difficulty that the proponents of reform had generating substantial support during this period had to do with the nature of the political coalition surrounding the issue. Urban members of Congress who controlled the relevant committees were mainly concerned with increasing the level of benefits, not the nature of the benefits, and they blocked any substantial changes to the programme even though polls showed that the public strongly favoured reforming the system.

The issue of fundamental welfare reform at last became an issue in the mid-1980s in the state of Wisconsin, a mid-sized state which rests between Chicago and the Canadian border. Wisconsin has a population of six-and-a-half million, with Milwaukee its largest city and about the same urban/ rural mix as the US average.

The essence of the reform movement which grew in Wisconsin incorporated the notion of mutual obligation of the state and the welfare recipient. As a result of reforms, today the state provides work opportunities for individuals of all capabilities, regardless of their current circumstances, and at the same time guarantees subsidised childcare and all other supports necessary for work.

> *'the reform movement which grew in Wisconsin incorporated the notion of mutual obligation of the state and the welfare recipient'*

An applicant for cash assistance is obligated, as a condition of receiving such assistance, to work in the private economy or, if work there is unavailable, at a full-time temporary job provided by the state. By this unremarkable trade-off, a rough balance is achieved between the contributions of the individual in need and the society which supports him.

The results of this trade-off, described in more detail below, are startling. In a nutshell, individuals who are able to work in the private economy find themselves better off by taking employment there, while those truly in need commit their full efforts to moving into the labour force as they contribute to society through temporary community service jobs. Equally importantly, the confidence of the general public in the welfare security system has been restored.

The Politics of Wisconsin Welfare Reform

The elevation of welfare to a major public issue in Wisconsin was caused by a Republican candidate for governor, Tommy Thompson, who ran for office against an incumbent on the issue of reforming the system. After a surprise victory, Thompson set about to make the changes he promised. Over the course of the next six years, from 1987 to 1993, Thompson submitted one or sometimes two reform proposals each year.

Most of these proposals would be seen as modest by today's standards, but they all struck a similar and consistent theme, that of personal responsibility. For example, one of his first proposals, 'Learnfare', required that, in order to receive a full assistance benefit, parents were obligated to ensure their children were present in school, reasoning that generations of children dropping their education was a cause of multi-generational dependency.

In order to implement the changes Thompson proposed, the state was required to submit a request for a waiver of federal welfare rules to Washington. The process of applying for consecutive waivers over a period of years, along with the publicity surrounding the proposals themselves, increased the political visibility of the welfare issue both in Wisconsin and in Washington. The public, in support of welfare reform from the beginning, rapidly endorsed ever more ambitious proposals and demanded that state legislators support the Governor.

As Democrat state legislators grew increasingly frustrated by the support for reform that the Governor had created through his series of proposals, they struck back. In December of 1993 the Democrats, in control of both houses of the state legislature, proposed the complete abolition of the federal welfare programme inside the state and its substitution with an undefined alternative to be worked out. Although some legislators were sincere in proposing this, the majority hoped that the proposal would precipitate a veto by the Republican Governor after which, the political point having been made, the Governor would be unable to assert his leadership on the issue.

Instead, Governor Thompson accepted the opportunity to design a work-based programme from the ground up, unconstrained by existing law and he signed the bill. He then set about his task in earnest, assembling a group of his staff and that of a conservative think-tank to develop a proposal.

The Philosophical Underpinnings of the Wisconsin Approach to Welfare Reform

The proposal resulting from the Governor's planning group was unique for two reasons. First, it was a complete substitution of the existing approach to helping the poor because there was no law remaining in place which had to be worked around. Secondly, resulting from the first, the new plan was based on a set of consistent philosophical principles which were mutually reinforcing. Some of these principles and their rationale are laid out below:

1. For those who can work, only work should pay:

   There are both economic and practical reasons for tying income to work. First, experience shows that entitlements to income without work have unwanted effects on dependency. In addition, it is essential that parents understand they will always be responsible for supporting themselves and their families through work: this influences behaviour and motivation in ongoing constructive ways. Finally, experience shows that individuals without extensive work history are usually in a stronger employment position after one or two years of actual work (at any wage) than after a comparable period of work preparation through education and training.

2. Begin with the assumption that everyone is capable of some kind of work:

The best way to help an individual who is out of work to get back into the labour force is to provide an actual work opportunity which matches their capabilities. This is contrary to many government subsidised 'helping' programmes which seek to identify barriers and limitations to work, and in so doing categorise and place individuals out of the reach of the workplace, where they might very well have succeeded if given the opportunity.

Only by testing the suitability of work through actual attempts to work can any true limitations which prevent full participation in the labour force be identified and resolved.

3. Strengthening the ability of parents to provide for their children is a better approach than having the government intervene directly on their behalf:

In well-meaning attempts to look after the interests of children, government has, over time, participated in many of the roles that were previously the exclusive responsibility of parents. There are many calls for government to take on still further responsibility for assuring the well-being of children.

However, government cannot raise children, only parents can. Government can do the most by helping to put parents in a position to meet their responsibilities, not by taking away these responsibilities for itself.

4. Measure the fairness of the new system by comparison with working families:

It is sometimes argued that a work-based welfare system will be unfair unless it can be shown that those formerly dependent on various benefit programmes will continue to receive a comparable package while working. Others argue that it is unrealistic to expect work for wages unless such wages will guarantee a high enough standard of living to make work seem worthwhile.

But self-sufficiency through work should be seen as an end in itself, quite apart from the package of benefits gained or lost as a result. More important is the relationship that those who are receiving welfare benefits have with those who are working to support themselves and their families in the low-wage economy and who have not asked for assistance.

5. Look to non-government organisations to deliver the programme:

It is axiomatic that government programmes, authorised by legislation, must be overseen by government as an agent of the public interest. However, for too long government has been the assumed operator of the programmes it devises. A more effective model is almost always for the government to set the ground rules and then let non-government entities actually operate programmes under public oversight.

The programme developed with the principles above in mind was passed into law and implemented with almost no change from its idealised conception. The plan has been operational for almost five years now, giving a true test of the impact, both positive and negative, of a radical work-based reform model.

The Wisconsin Works Programme (W2)

Wisconsin's new welfare programme, called Wisconsin Works, or W2, offers those who need assistance to provide for themselves and their families any one of four work options. The former 'entitlement' to income without work has been withdrawn, and replaced with this offer of benefits earned through full-time work, available for individuals of all capabilities. So long as adults asking for assistance are willing to work, income and other supports will be provided to meet the needs of the family.

Wisconsin Works offices are similar to former welfare offices except that they incorporate both income support and employment functions inside one agency and through a single caseworker who meets with applicants. An individual coming to a W2 office asking for income assistance is met by one of these caseworkers who talks through the options available.

If the individual is not disabled, four work options are available (disabled applicants are sent for a disability review). The preferred solution is to have an applicant look for and accept the best available private employment opportunity. The W2 agency obtains private job referrals and makes these available along with assistance in looking for work and preparing for work interviews. Only if sincere efforts to find private employment are unsuccessful, will other work options be considered by the caseworker as alternatives.

Unlike the incentives in other traditional welfare programmes, the applicant to W2 has every incentive to accept private employment if offered. This is because full-time work is always required as a condition of receiving W2 benefits, and private employment always pays more than any of the other subsidised work options.

Private employment for low-wage work in the US is supported in several ways. The US current minimum wage of $5.15 per hour is supplemented by a federal tax credit which goes to all low-income individuals working full-time at low wages. The tax credit is worth up to about $4,000 per year for very low earners with large families, decreasing from there. Therefore an individual earning the minimum of about $10,500 in the private economy will actually take home an amount closer to $14,000 when the credit is added.*

If private unsubsidised employment is unavailable, the second option for the same applicant is a subsidised private job. The wage subsidies, paid by the state to the private employer, are intended to partially offset some of the extra supervisory costs associated with helping to train and teach

---

* Few individuals earn the minimum wage at the current time, with market forces having increased low-end wages to over $6.00 per hour in most places and $7.00 per hour in high-wage urban areas.

a novice employee how to be productive in a given work setting. In actual fact, the number of individuals in subsidised private jobs under W2 is quite small, largely because the market demand for employees is so strong that most applicants, even inexperienced ones, are able to find regular unsubsidised employment.

After attempts to find employment in the private labour market have been shown to be unsuccessful, a third option is a fully subsidised community service job or 'CSJ'. These fully subsidised jobs are usually provided by government agencies. The job-holders provide useful services to the agencies and the public, while being managed and trained by regular supervisors on-site. Such jobs may include telephone answering or filing in an office, working outside in the parks and recreation department, acting as a teacher's aide or a nurse's assistant, or any number of other options. The organisations providing the work opportunities must guarantee that they are not substituting CSJ workers for regular employees, and they must provide good supervision in exchange for the additional work provided to their agencies by CSJ workers.

In places where CSJs are heavily used, currently in Wisconsin but also in New York City, agencies using CSJ employees find that the additional benefits from the labour contribution to their organisation's output more than makes up for the supervisory and other costs associated with providing the temporary job opportunities.

A challenge which must be overcome by a system such as this is that CSJs, if not properly managed, can become long-term substitutes for private employment. The W2 system assures that this will not occur because the CSJs pay $673 per month, substantially less than private employment even at the minimum wage. In addition, W2 ensures that other benefits, such as subsidised childcare, are available to all low-income workers, not just those inside the W2 system. Therefore there is no incentive for those seeking assistance to remain in subsidised CSJs any longer than is necessary.

The fourth and final work option is called a transitional job and is available for those who are not fully able to work in a CSJ assignment for reasons relating to physical or mental health. Typical reasons for needing a transitional assignment include the presence of mild disability or recovery from alcoholism or drug abuse. Transitional jobs often are set up in sheltered workshops where simple tasks are made part of the work assignment, and vocational rehabilitation, substance abuse treatment, or additional training is often incorporated.

> *'fears that many individuals and families would be unable to cope with the new obligations appear to be unfounded'*

With these four work options—unsubsidised employment, subsidised private employment, community service work and transitional work—almost everyone receiving benefits is working to support themselves and their family.

Results from Wisconsin Works

The Wisconsin system resolves the major issue confronting policy makers over the design of income security systems, namely how to ensure universal coverage while maximising movement into the private economy and minimising long-term dependency.

The results from five years of programme operations prove the feasibility of the system, whose impact has exceeded the highest hopes of its designers. Moreover, fears that many individuals and families would be unable to cope with the new obligations appear to be unfounded.

Research conducted by the University of Wisconsin, which tracked individuals enrolled in W2 over the two-year period of 1998 and 1999, shows substantial economic progress by those participating in the programme. More than 70 per cent of those who enrolled in W2 were out of the programme just 24 months later, mostly employed in the private economy. As a result, caseloads within Wisconsin dropped dramatically over a short two-year period, from about 65,000 cases statewide to fewer than 17,000.

Earnings for those who worked rose from $5,600 to $7,650 in just one year (full- and part-time workers averaged together). This jump in earned income of over a third in such a short period results from a combination of increases in both wages and number of hours worked. And when other earnings such as food stamps and child support paid by absent fathers are included, average family income rose from \$12,100 to \$14,800 (with still additional income provided to most of these families through the tax credit subsidy to low-wage workers).

Critics of Wisconsin Works say the programme is too demanding. However, there is little or no evidence that the programme has created collateral problems among the eligible population. The rate of referrals to the system which cares for neglected or abused children is down over the period since the introduction of W2, and child support collections from absent fathers are up. There is no overall change in the number of individuals using the homeless shelter system or free food pantries.

Conclusion

This paper has described the main philosophical underpinnings of Wisconsin Works and its main programmatic solution to the problem of dependency. Several other innovations have been incorporated into the programme design as well. Two such innovations, the privatisation of the programme delivery system and the substitution of performance contracting for the regulatory command-and-control administrative system have been included to assure that the programme is delivered effectively and as intended.

In May 2002, when this chapter was going to press, the House of the US Congress passed a bill which adopts as national policy many of the provisions contained in the Wisconsin plan.[1] The agency which administers the national welfare programme, the US Department of Health and Human Services (HHS) is headed by former Wisconsin Governor Tommy Thompson, who came to the President's attention through his welfare innovations. Thus we can be assured that the Wisconsin model of reform will continue to influence US welfare policy, and as the other authors in this publication attest, may also be applicable to other European countries experiencing increases in welfare dependency.

Moral Arguments for Welfare Reform

Alan Deacon

There is no one moral case for welfare reform. Instead, the literature offers a range of arguments about what should be the nature and direction of reform. Four such arguments are outlined briefly in this paper.

The paper starts from the premise that these arguments reflect conflicting views of what constitutes a good society and what role welfare can play in bringing such a society into being. Each offers a different perspective on what should be the role and purpose of welfare. They are not mutually exclusive, but each draws upon and articulates a different understanding of human nature and of the relationship between welfare and human behaviour and motivation. The writers whose work is outlined briefly below all begin with the premise that, in James Q. Wilson's words, human beings possess 'a set of traits and predispositions that limits what we may do and suggests guides to what we must do'. Nevertheless, they have very different views of what these 'traits and predispositions' are, and of the ways in which they constrain and guide welfare policy.[1]

- **Welfare should express and encourage altruism**. This perspective assumes that the creation of a more equal and cohesive society will foster a sense of mutual obligation and will help to realise the moral potentialities of its citizens. The task of welfare is to redistribute resources and opportunities, and thereby provide a framework for the encouragement and expression of altruism.

- **Welfare should act as a channel for the pursuit of self-interest**. This perspective assumes the overwhelm-

ing majority of people who claim welfare will act ratio-
nally to better the conditions of themselves and their
dependants. The task of welfare is to provide a framework of incentives that channels this desire for self-
improvement in ways conducive to the common good.

- **Welfare should exercise authority over the dependent.** This perspective starts from the premise that a
significant proportion of claimants lack the capacities to
pursue their own self interest. In consequence they do not
respond to changes in the framework of incentives in the
way that the previous perspective assumes. The task of
welfare is to compel such people to act in ways that are
conducive to their long-term betterment, and hence to the
common good.

- **Welfare should act as a mechanism for moral
regeneration.** This perspective starts from the assumption that people are also motivated by a sense of commitment, and by an acceptance that they have obligations to
the communities in which they live. The task of welfare
is to foster and enhance this sense of duty, and it should
look to do so through persuasion and moral argument.

There are three points that need to be made before each
perspective is examined in turn.

- There is a clear and immediate difference between the
first perspective and the three that follow. This is that
the first perspective views the central task of welfare as
being to reduce inequality, the other three view the
central task as to reduce dependency. The first is primarily concerned with the distribution of resources, the other
three are primarily concerned with the way people
behave.

- European debates on welfare were long dominated by the
first perspective. The extent of this domination is a
matter of dispute, as is the degree to which it was reflected in the policies that were adopted by governments.
What is clear, however, is that the other three perspectives were consciously developed as critiques of the first.
Moreover, the collective impact of these critiques has

been to fragment the welfare debate and to place the question of how welfare influences behaviour higher on the academic and political agenda.

• There are still important differences between US and European interpretations of the term 'welfare'. It the US it refers to means-tested cash assistance paid primarily to lone mothers and their children. In Europe it traditionally referred to a broad range of benefits and services. In recent years, however, commentators and politicians in Europe have adopted the American usage, especially when discussing so-called welfare-to-work schemes.

Welfare and Altruism

This perspective is closely associated with the English ethical socialist Richard Titmuss.[2] Titmuss started from the premise that people are often motivated by a regard for the concerns and needs of others. He argued that the primary purpose of welfare is to foster and encourage these feelings of altruism and to give expression to them. In order to fulfil this purpose, however, welfare must first contribute to a broader redistribution of resources and opportunities. This is because a reduction in social inequalities is a pre-condition for the creation of a common culture and for the establishment of social relationships based upon altruism. Moreover, this redistribution can and must be achieved through social services which are themselves non-discriminatory and which foster a sense of community. At the heart of Titmuss's perspective, then, is the belief that resources must be channelled to the poor within an infrastructure of benefits and services that are open to and used by all. As far as possible, entitlement to welfare should be universal and unconditional. It should not depend upon the incomes of claimants, and claimants should not be required to meet conditions regarding their behaviour or their character.

It followed that Titmuss was bitterly hostile to judgementalism in welfare. He did not rule out the possibility that there was a small minority of people whose poverty could be attributed to their own behaviour, at least in part. In the 1930s he had been sympathetic to the idea that there was a social problem group and in his later work Titmuss acknowledged that welfare systems had to avoid 'building in disincentives to full-time work and disincentives to the stability of marriage and family responsibilities'. In general, however, he argued that these concerns do not affect the 'rights of the consumer to certain services irrespective of their morals and patterns of behaviour'.[3]

This reflected Titmuss's optimism regarding human nature. It must be stressed that this optimism did not emerge in the 1960s but was a prominent feature of his early writings. *Parents Revolt*, for example, was published in 1942. Co-written with Kay Titmuss, this claimed that the decline in the birth rate represented a rejection of the 'virus of acquisitiveness' that was engendered by capitalism. There could be no solution to the problems posed by a declining population, they argued, so long as 'each individual follows his own interests, is taught to serve himself and not others, and is forced by the character of the environment in which he moves to act acquisitively and not co-operatively'. What was needed were new values that 'will release that deep, long-frustrated desire in man to serve humanity and not self'.[4]

By far the most influential expression of this argument, however, came in Titmuss's last book, *The Gift Relationship*. In this book Titmuss contrasted the National Blood Transfusion Service (NBTS) in Britain with the operation of commercial markets for blood in other countries, particularly the United States. He claimed to have demonstrated that the blood supplied by voluntary donors was far superior in terms of its purity and the dependability of its supply than that obtained from commercial donors.

For Titmuss, the all-important point was that those who donated to the NBTS in Britain were 'free not to give'. They could 'have behaved differently'.

> Their decisions were not determined by structure or by function or controlled by ineluctable historical forces. They were not compelled, coerced, bribed or paid to give.[5]

That they chose to give was due to the way in which the National Health Service 'allowed and encouraged sentiments of altruism, reciprocity and social duty to express themselves'. This, said Titmuss, was but one example of how social policy could 'facilitate the expression of man's moral sense', and thereby 'help to actualize the social and moral potentialities of all citizens'.[6]

Titmuss died in 1973, and in subsequent years socialist thinking on welfare became increasingly preoccupied with the growth of material inequalities and paid correspondingly less attention to altruism and the quality of social relationships. Because it paid less attention to altruism it also paid less attention than Titmuss had done to the question of how far people's behaviours and activities represented some form of meaningful choice. Titmuss's rejection of individualist or behavioural accounts of poverty hardened and broadened into a more determinist approach that, in effect, precluded any discussion of such factors.

Welfare and Self-interest

At the heart of this perspective is the belief that the rules and regulations which govern entitlement to benefits and services must reward those activities and attributes which should be encouraged and penalise those which need to be discouraged. If they do not do this, then they will lead people to behave in ways which damage themselves and the communities in which they live.

The argument that welfare does indeed generate such 'perverse incentives' is associated most closely with the American conservative Charles Murray.[7] As Steve Teles has observed, there 'is no way to overestimate the effect' that the publication of Murray's book *Losing Ground* had upon 'the intellectual debate on poverty' in the US.[8] It shifted the focus and transformed the tone of that debate, and had an important if less direct impact in Britain.

In essence, Murray argued that the growth in welfare dependency in the late 1960s and 1970s was due to the ways in which the expansion of welfare under the War on Poverty changed the behaviour of the poor.

There were two components of the case that Charles Murray presented in *Losing Ground*. The first was an assertion about data, a statement about trends in poverty and other indicators of social pathology. The second was his interpretation of that data, his explanation of those trends. In consequence, the book gave rise to two parallel but discrete debates; one about the accuracy and validity of the evidence Murray provided and the other about the plausibility of his analyses of whatever changes had occurred.

> The most compelling explanation for the marked shift in the fortunes of the poor is that they continued to respond, as they always had, to the world as they found it, but that we—meaning the not-poor and un-disadvantaged—had changed the rules of their world.[9]

Murray's experiences working for Peace Corps and the United States Agency for International Development in Thailand had made him aware that behaviour which seemed rational to government planners often made no sense whatsoever to people living in the rural villages. The same gulf existed between the American poor and the policy makers in Washington. Those who planned the War on Poverty failed to recognise that 'the behaviours that are "rational" are different at different economic levels'.

'behaviours that are rational are different at different economic levels'

> I begin with the proposition that all, poor and non-poor alike, use the same general calculus in arriving at decisions; only the exigencies are different. Poor people play with fewer chips and cannot wait as long for results. Therefore they tend to reach decisions that a more affluent person would not reach.[10]

This meant, said Murray, that there was no need to 'invoke the spectres of cultural pathology or inferior upbringing' to explain dependency. It was just a case of people 'responding to the reality of the world around them'.

Charles Murray's assumptions about the centrality and legitimacy of self interest are shared by Frank Field, who served as Minister for Welfare Reform in the first 'New Labour' government in Britain.[11] Field has written, for example, that the 'sanitised, post-Christian view of human character held by Titmuss' was 'built on sand' because the 'fallen side of mankind' was simply 'written out' of the script.

It is not a question of seeking the means by which the values of individuals are changed. It is rather a question of setting a legal framework where natural decent instincts guided by self-interest are allowed to operate in a manner which enhances the common good.... Set the right framework and the moral improvement (which I would prefer to call an increase in well-being) will take place.[12]

More than anything else, 'setting the right framework' means reducing the role of the means test within welfare. By their very nature, means tests penalise those who save or increase their incomes, and thereby discourage the very behaviours that should be encouraged. Unlike Murray, Field is seeking to restructure welfare, not to abolish it. His proposals for social insurance will cost money, not save it. This means that the scope of his analyses is necessarily broader. Whereas Murray could take it as read that a majority of the American public would believe it to be in their own interest to cut back on the welfare paid to the poor, Field has to devise ways of securing popular support for the welfare reforms he is proposing. In his case, welfare has to channel the self-interest not just of the poor but of the electorate as well.

To date, this has proved to be Field's Achilles' heel. In office he was unable to convince his fellow ministers—and especially the Chancellor Gordon Brown—that it was possible to reduce the scope of the means test in the British welfare system. Nevertheless, Field's contribution remains significant in the development of New Labour thinking on welfare. Encouraged by Tony Blair to 'think the unthinkable', Field did more than anyone on the centre-left to challenge the dominance of the Titmuss school and to align New Labour with an older working-class tradition of self-improvement and mutual aid.

Welfare and Authority

According to this perspective, the explanation of long-term poverty lies not in the perverse incentives generated by welfare but in the character of the poor themselves and in a political culture that condones self-destructive behaviour. It follows that the solution is to be found not in the creation of new opportunities or financial inducements but in the exercise of authority. The role of welfare should be to compel the poor to behave in ways that are conducive to their long-term betterment, and thereby promote the common good. This can be achieved most readily by making their entitlement to benefits and services conditional upon their behaving in prescribed ways. The most obvious and important example of such conditionality is, of course, the imposition of work requirements upon applicants for unemployment benefits—otherwise known as workfare. Advocates of the so-called New Paternalism, however, argue that it also offers a remedy for other ways in which underclass families are allegedly failing to function. If it is feasible to compel welfare mothers to work, then why not also require them to attend high school or to keep off drugs? In addition, they can be required to ensure that their children attend school regularly, or that their children receive the immunisation injections they need.

By far the most important advocate of the New Paternalism is another American conservative, Lawrence Mead.[13] 'The entire tradition' of tackling poverty and dependency through 'incentives or disincentives', Mead argues, is 'bankrupt'. He rejects outright what he calls the 'competence assumption'—the assumption that the individual is willing and able to advance his or her own economic interests. In repudiation of Murray, he insists that 'the disincentives of welfare' are 'insufficient to explain the extent of nonwork and female-headed households' among the poor. Furthermore, it is an 'abuse of language' to describe such behaviour as rational since rationality must involve foresight.

The long-term poor are the 'dutiful but defeated' who require paternalistic direction. In this sense, the rationale for the new paternalism is underpinned by some very old political ideas. It is the argument, derived from Aristotle, that the development of moral character requires self discipline and the acquisition of good habits. People become virtuous by the practice of virtue. They acquire self-control by the exercise of self-control. It is precisely this process that can be undermined by unconditional or indiscriminate welfare, but which can be reinforced by the supervision and direction provided by paternalistic welfare.

Even so there remains a question mark over the long-term effects of paternalistic direction. By definition paternalism means treating the dependent poor like children, not in itself the most obvious way of promoting self-reliance and self-discipline. What happens when the direction ceases? Mead himself recognises that if paternalism is to be truly effective then it will have to lead to changes in the culture of low-income communities. There will have to be a new consensus that fosters and inculcates the values of responsibility and self-reliance. Government paternalism, he concedes, was not needed in the past on anything like the scale he now advocates precisely because such values were upheld by informal networks and private forms of social control.

> It is possible that public paternalism might help regenerate those informal controls, partly by involving community organizations in directive programs and partly by legitimizing the idea—in and outside government—that social norms can and should be enforced.[14]

It is at this point that the boundary between paternalism and the more conservative forms of communitarianism becomes somewhat blurred.

Welfare and Obligation

Some argue that the central objective of welfare should be to foster and enhance a sense of duty and of commitment. From this perspective, welfare should look primarily to persuasion rather than to compulsion, to encouragement and to moral argument rather than to financial inducements or penalties. Such arguments are associated most closely with communitarianism. As Amitai Etzioni notes, a prominent theme of recent communitarian writing is that 'much of social conduct is, and that more ought to be, sustained and guided by an informal web of social bonds and moral voices of the community'. These new or so-called 'responsive' communitarians have sought to demonstrate that it is both desirable and possible to 'rely first and foremost on attempts to persuade, rather than coerce, people when seeking to promote pro-social behaviour'.[15]

Modern communitarianism emerged in the 1980s as a response to what its advocates saw as the excessive individualism of contemporary western societies. Its central claim is that this excessive individualism has produced a profound and damaging imbalance. Far too much attention is paid to the rights of individuals, the enjoyment of which safeguards their freedom and enhances their personal autonomy. Far too little attention is paid to the social responsibilities of those individuals, the acceptance of which maintains social order and enhances the communities in which they live. The literature on communitarianism is now large and diverse. At is core, however, are three much older beliefs.

• that liberty is not licence, and that the former requires a measure of self-restraint on the part of individuals.

• that it is possible to speak of a common good, which can be identified and pursued through collective deliberation and action.

• that individuals possess a moral sense, which disposes them to make moral judgements and to heed the moral judgements of others.

The communitarian ideal is what Etzioni calls a normative moral order. This is a society in which order is maintained by appeals to common values and by moral argument, rather than by economic incentives or the exercise of authority. How far such a society is possible depends upon the degree of tension that exists between that which people would like to do—their preferences—and that which they are required to do—their commitments or their duties. The more people accept their duties as reasonable, the more they share a commitment to a set of core values, then the more the social order can be based upon 'normative means'.

Shared values are quite different from intellectual positions that have been agreed after debate or negotiation. They are values that have been 'internalised'; that is, they have become part of the person and have been incorporated into his or her inner self and help shape his or her preferences. These values also have to be embedded in the four social formations that shape behaviour: the family, the school, the community, and the wider community of communities. These social formations constitute what Etzioni calls the moral infrastructure.

The role that Etzioni envisages this moral infrastructure can play in sustaining a normative social order reflects the assumptions he makes about human nature. Almost inevitably, he suggests that communitarian thinking rests upon a 'third view' which is distinct from both the liberal assumption that human nature is essentially benign and capable of being perfected and the conservative assumption that it is brutish and in need of restraint and direction. This 'third view' is a 'dynamic' or 'developmental' one. It holds that people are indeed born basically savage but that they can 'become much more virtuous'. Quite how virtuous they can become will depend on the extent to which values are internalised and embedded in the moral infrastructure.

There is, however, a further constraint. Societies that rely upon voluntary commitment must be responsive to the realities of human nature. They cannot espouse 'heroic moral agendas' which ask too much of both individual citizens and the moral infrastructure. Within this 'particular limit', however, the social formations have the potential to transform the 'barbarian at birth' into the communitarian citizen.

There are four broad themes of what may be loosely termed a communitarian approach to welfare reform.

- The first and most obvious is an emphasis upon the obligations as well as the rights of those who claim welfare. In practice this means that welfare benefits should be conditional. Support for conditionality is not, of course, confined to communitarians. For communitarians, however, these obligations are much broader and more deeply rooted. They reflect the fact that individuals are not autonomous selves but are socially embedded in communities.

- A second theme is the need to build popular support for welfare. This reflects communitarianism's commitment to a voluntary moral order, and its assumption that effective communities can only be created through what the Responsive Communitarian Platform called 'genuine public conviction'.

- A third theme is that welfare must be judgemental and moralistic. Communitarians reject the non-judgemental- ism of Titmuss and the quasi-Titmuss paradigm* on the grounds that it stifles the moral voice of the community.

- Above all, communitarian welfare would not take people as it found them, but would try to change them. It would seek to shape their values and mould their characters. In Jonathan Sacks's words, it would employ 'a wider reper- toire of policies than those which rely exclusively on coercive legislation, economic incentive, or direct govern- ment control'. Instead, it would focus on 'character and on the institutions that promote a strong sense of person- hood and social concern'.[16]

Communitarianism shares with paternalism the belief that a central objective of welfare is to enforce social norms and expectations. Where the two perspectives differ sharply is over the methods by which welfare should seek to do this. The paternalist perspective is essentially a short-term strategy. It is prepared to exercise control and direction over the lives of poor people in order to force them to change their behaviour. Even its staunchest advocates, however, acknowledge that they can offer no assurance that any change in behaviour will be maintained once this direction has stopped. In contrast, the communitarian perspective is a strategy for the longer term. It seeks to persuade people

---

*   The term quasi-Titmuss paradigm is used to refer to the ideas, values and assumptions that dominated centre-left thinking on welfare in the 1970s and 1980s. It differed from Titmuss's own position in its neglect of issues of human agency. It explained social pathologies entirely in terms of social structures and social divisions based primarily on social class.

to change their behaviour through moral arguments expressed by and on behalf of the community. Even its staunchest advocates, however, acknowledge that the requisite changes in the moral infrastructure will take time.

Conclusion

The perspectives outlined here are not discrete. Nor does any one of them correspond to the programme of a particular political party. Indeed, in the British context, it is the claim of New Labour that its much vaunted 'third way' is eclectic, and that it draws upon and reconciles approaches hitherto seen as antagonistic.[17] Nevertheless, the perspectives do reflect conflicting views of what is the proper role of government in general and welfare policy in particular. In this respect they represent distinctive and important moral arguments for welfare reform.

Welfare Reform:
The Netherlands

Hans Hoogervorst

'**D**on't rock the boat' is a typical expression for the conservative way of thinking: no sudden, wild manoeuvering, or the boat will get damaged. Navigate calmly, because even the smallest of changes in course will lead to an entirely different destination.

Very prudent, of course. But only on condition that the look-out posts are well manned, that there is a wary eye for changing circumstances and that we hoist the sails to keep ourselves on the right course.

This is the image that presents itself to me when I think about the future of the welfare state in Holland.

The Netherlands has experienced a period of great prosperity. The economy has grown considerably and, in its tow, so have employment opportunities. For the first time since the 1960s, the Netherlands has been confronted with labour market shortages. The number of unemployed has decreased and the rise in prosperity has been felt by almost everyone. Prospects have improved further thanks to the European market.

So, we are doing well, but the welfare state in the Netherlands and in Europe only has a future if we persist in keeping a keen eye on our surroundings and never forget that social policy starts and ends with employment. A comparison with the United States also makes it clear there is no reason for a self-indulgent attitude in Europe. If we set the average US GDP *per capita* at 100, the average GDP *per*

Based on a speech given by the Dutch Secretary of State for Social Affairs and Employment, Hans Hoogervorst, to the Stockholm Network/Edmund Burke Foundation, 1 February, 2002, the Hague, Netherlands.

Figure 1: GDP Per Capita, 2001

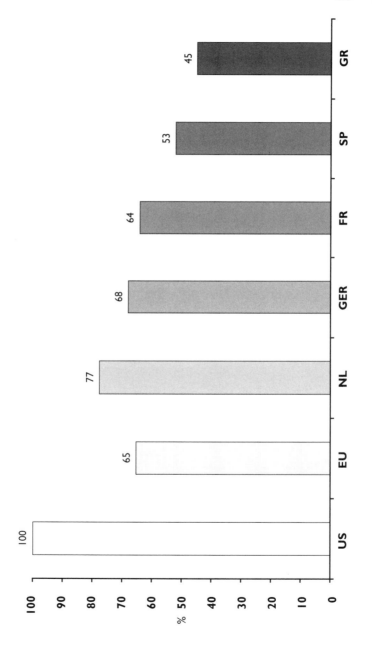

26

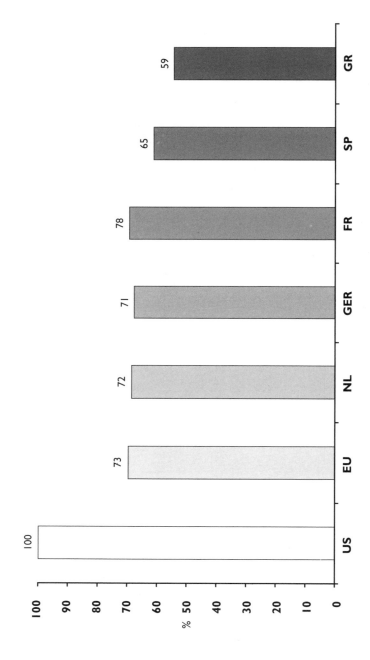

Figure 2: Difference in Labour Productivity

capita in the EU as a whole would be 65 (Figure 1, p. 25). Within the EU there are considerable differences. With 77 per cent, the Netherlands has a high EU ranking. Germany and France score more or less around the average. Spain and Greece still lag behind, but are catching up. The conclusion is clear: prosperity in the US is on a higher level than in the EU.

Many will point to the fact that income distribution in the US is much less even than in Europe. That is true. Poverty in the US is a more severe problem than in most European countries. In the European welfare state, the emphasis is more on social security. That has clear advantages in terms of social protection. But there seems to be a trade-off with economic dynamism. Also, it is clear that the majority of American people enjoy higher living standards than people in Europe.

An important reason for the difference in prosperity is the higher rate of labour market participation in the US. In 2001, the participation rate in full-time equivalent in the US was 72 per cent. In the EU as a whole, this rate was 58 per cent. In the Netherlands it was 57 per cent. In Germany and France, 59 per cent. In the UK and Sweden it was slightly higher: 62 and 65 per cent respectively.

In addition, people in the US work longer hours than in the EU. The average in the US is 1,869 working hours per year. In the Netherlands it is only 1,343 working hours. The higher labour market participation and the longer working hours alone explain two-thirds of the difference in prosperity.

The second important factor for this difference is the higher labour productivity in the US. If we set American labour productivity at 100, you can see that the average labour productivity in the EU scores an average of 73 (Figure 2, p. 26). The Netherlands and Germany score about this average. France is above average and Spain and Greece are below it.

These figures are self explanatory. And given the considerable differences between the individual European countries, they also point to a third, more general explanation for the difference in prosperity between the EU and the US: the considerable dynamics of the homogenous American market. If we compare these dynamics and homogeneity with the EU we can see that the European market is in some aspects still in its infancy.

Recently, I read an article which explained that a Dutch person who wishes to buy a new car is better off booking a holiday trip to Denmark. The difference in car prices between the Netherlands and Denmark are such that he can easily afford this holiday from the profit. The cause: when setting the net price of a car, producers keep the relevant taxes in mind. The higher the tax level, the lower the price.

This is an example of an imperfect market, a market that still has a lot of barriers and regulations between the various EU countries.

Our first glance across the frontiers offers a clear view. Europe is lagging behind the US in a number of ways. In the field of labour market participation, working hours and labour productivity. But also in the field of market forces.

There is a growing awareness in Europe that we need to catch up with the United States in terms of economic competitiveness. This will have consequences for the European concept of the welfare state.

There are three major challenges for the future:

1 Improving the international competitive position of Europe.

2 Dealing with the issue of ageing in connection with the pensions issue.

3 The consequences of immigration within the EU.

1 The International Competitive Position of Europe

A good competitive position is essential to the future of Europe. This position is under pressure. For this reason, new strategic goals for Europe were set out in Lisbon: before 2010, the EU must become the most competitive and dynamic knowledge economy in the world, capable of sustainable economic growth, with more and better jobs and stronger social cohesion. This is a truly ambitious programme that requires efforts to be made in many fields.

The Lisbon goals are lofty and ambitious, but when it comes to putting them into practice old habits die hard. We have seen nothing like the far-reaching liberalisation that Commissioner Bolkestein is striving for. It is disappointing that the member states cannot follow the pace of the European Commission.

2. Dealing with the Issue of Ageing in Connection with the Pension Issue

The second major challenge to the welfare state is the consequences of an ageing population. In Europe we are sitting on a slowly ticking time bomb. If that time bomb is not defused, we will suffer great damage.

There are two significant phenomena: fewer young people and an ageing population. Fewer young people, because fewer children are being born; ageing, because the number of elderly people is rising sharply. Moreover, the average citizen is not just living longer but elderly people make up a larger proportion of the population. So what we have here is in fact double ageing.

There is a considerable increase in the percentage of elderly people over 65 in relation to the working part of the population between 20 and 64 years old: the so-called elderly dependency ratio.

Figure 3 (p. 30) is clear. The right bar shows that the EU average will rise from 27 per cent in the year 2002 to 44 per cent in the year 2030. In other words: at this moment, about 75 per cent of the European population is still working, thus earning an income for all of us. In 2030, this will be down to almost half of the population. Now, three employed Europeans jointly finance the pension of one senior European. By 2030, every employed European will have his own elderly person to provide for. And this is a mere EU average.

The big question, obviously, is whether we will still be able to finance old-age provision in Europe in the near future without getting ourselves into major financial or social problems.

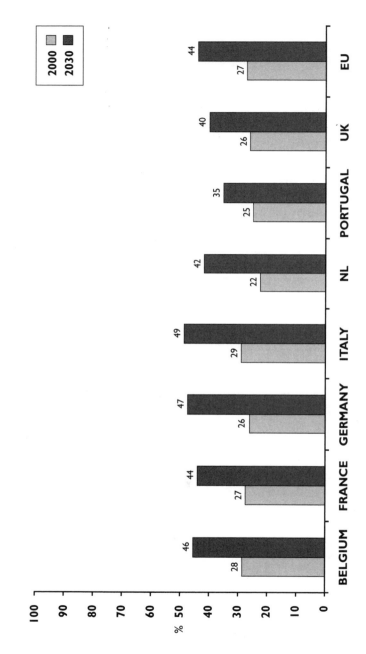

Figure 3: Elderly Dependency Ratios in Europe, 65+: 20-64

The question is even more compelling because no less than 88 per cent of all European pensions are financed by means of the pay-as-you-go system: this means that the tax payer pays for the pension benefits of the elderly.

Figures 4 and 5 illustrate what the financial consequences of this situation will be for a number of individual member states.

Over the next 30 years, we will see a sharp increase in the built-up pension rights of the over-25s in all countries (Fig. 4, p. 32). In 1990, these rights already amounted to 157 per cent of Italy's GDP. In 2030 they will rise to 207 per cent. In Germany this percentage will increase from 138 to 186 per cent, and in the Netherlands from 103 to 144 per cent.

Figure 5 (p. 33) shows the capital saved for pensions in the same countries. The amount of saved capital in the Netherlands is vast: in 1999 it was 141 per cent of GDP. Many other countries are nowhere near this. Italy for instance has only 19 per cent of GDP, Germany has 12 per cent, France has just six per cent and Spain four per cent of GDP.

If nothing is done to change this situation, a doom scenario threatens for those countries, in which fewer shoulders will have to carry an ever-increasing burden. It has been calculated that the result of an unchanged policy within the European member states will either lead to a situation in which the level of old-age pensions will be brought down by half, or that contributions will have to be doubled up to 25 per cent of people's income.

'fewer shoulders will have to carry an ever-increasing burden'

The possible consequences are not difficult to guess. Increasing wage costs, increasing social contributions, decreasing consumption, faltering competitive strength, increasing unemployment, a growing state debt, higher inflation. Not all of these plagues of Egypt will befall us, but it will be extremely difficult to avoid them all.

Fortunately there is still time to take action to defuse the ticking time bomb. But we will have to act now.

32

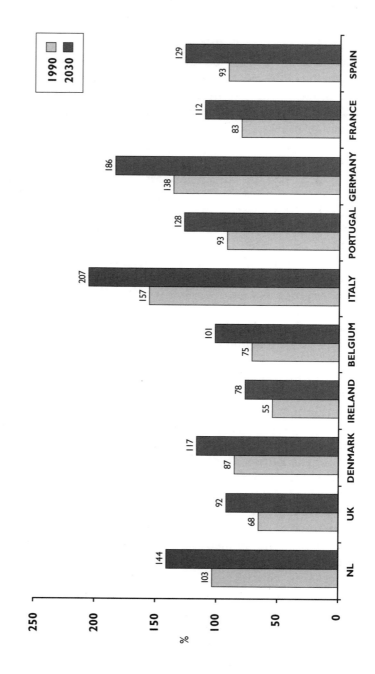

Figure 4: Increasing Pension Rights in Pay-As-You-Go System, Expressed as % of GDP

Figure 5: Saved Capital 1999 Expressed as % of GDP

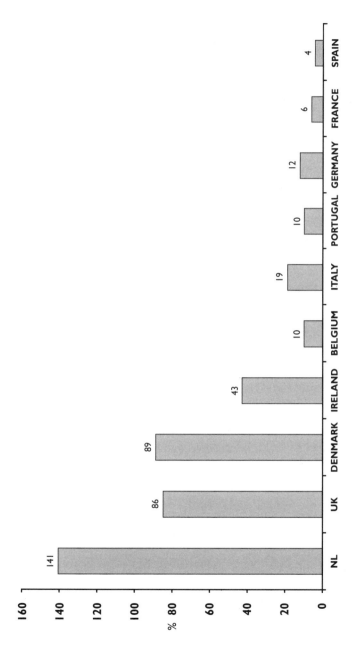

How? For instance, by making savings for future pension benefits in a way similar to the Dutch pension model. And if that does not work, by helping people to find a job and especially to keep on working for longer. And, of course, the most simple solution: bringing down the size of public debt. For the same reason, the rules of the stability pact cannot be relaxed.

3. The Consequences of Immigration into the EU

The third factor that poses a challenge to the European welfare state is the increasing immigration of people into the EU from outside Europe. Often low-skilled and unable to speak the language, a large portion of these immigrants end up depending on the welfare schemes of their host EU country.

Is this their inevitable lot or is there an alternative? The US was created by immigrants and can even now absorb a great number of immigrants, most of whom find their way to the job market.

In Europe, on the contrary, many immigrants have grown dependent on the welfare state over the past decades. There is simply not enough room for low-skilled labour. They, as well as their children, become out of touch with society, while immigrants in particular need this contact most. In the past few years, fortunately, many immigrants in the Netherlands have managed to find a job, through intense labour market politics, considerable efforts in education, and most of all because of the lasting economic boom. But immigrants are still at a disadvantage and the pressure of immigration persists. The welfare state will have to adapt by becoming more active.

> 'The welfare state will have to adapt by becoming more active'

We will have to face a number of major challenges if we want to safeguard the European welfare state. The major social challenge is activation. More people should get into employment—the unemployed, the elderly and immigrants. Only then will the Lisbon strategy stand a chance of success, only then can we defuse the pension time bomb and offer a better prospect to immigrants. Obviously, the social challenge will for the greater part be the task of the individual member states.

What Can the Netherlands Do?

Let us first have a look at developments over the past few years. Our state budgetary deficit of minus 5.1 per cent of GDP in 1990 has turned into a surplus. The state debt too diminished spectacularly from 79.2 per cent of GDP in 1990 to 51.8 per cent of GDP in 2001.

And finally, there has been growth of employment. In the past six years, employment opportunities have grown at an average of 2.6 per cent per annum, which is far more than in the US (1.4 per cent).

In short, the Dutch economy and public finances have improved markedly in the last decade. But not enough. There are still people on the sidelines. People are not always sufficiently stimulated to accept work, even though the opportunities are abundant. And economic growth does not come along all by itself either. In other words, there are still a number of pitfalls.

Increasing wage costs affect our competitive position. Since 1997, the competitive position of the Netherlands has deteriorated. Figure 6 (p. 36) shows the development of wage costs per unit product. By now, the downturn totals 11.3 per cent as compared to our major competitors. This is worrying, because the growth of employment in the Netherlands has for the most part resulted from a moderate wage development.

Another pitfall is the Dutch disablement scheme act (WAO). It is of the essence that people in the WAO who are able to work should actually do so. Also, it is essential that the influx into the WAO is stemmed. Holland is one of the most healthy nations in the world, but also one of the countries with the highest number of occupational disabled people in the world. So something is not right. More strict admission rules to the WAO and, in addition, financial incentives for employers and employees are absolutely necessary.

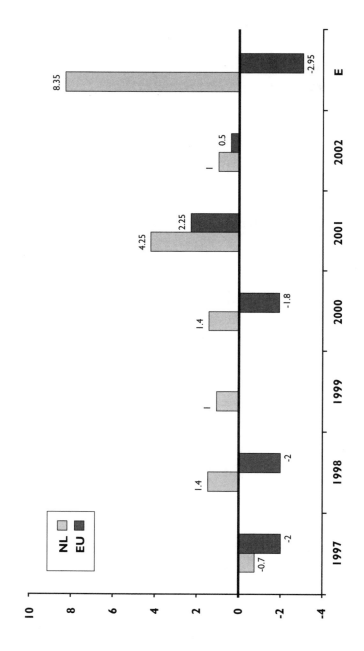

Figure 6: Development Wage Costs Per Unit Product, 1997-2002

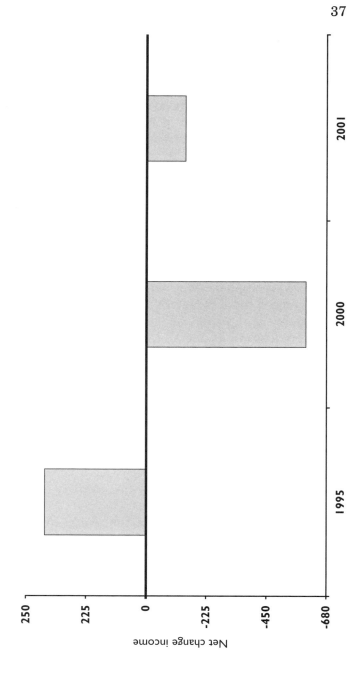

Figure 7: Transition from Welfare to Employment (singles) in 1995, 2000 and 2001

There is also the poverty trap. In Holland, there are a number of provisions that help people who are on welfare to make ends meet. For instance, subsidies on rents or municipal income provisions, such as rules that exempt them from local taxes. These are sound regulations in the field of focused income support. But there is a drawback.

The moment a single person, a single parent or a couple accept a job at the minimum wage, they lose out financially. As you can see from Figure 7 (p. 37), there was still some progress in 1995. In 2002, this profit proves to have turned into a setback. And even in 2001, after we had already taken the necessary measures, the setback was still there. Only when earnings exceed the minimum wage by 110, 130 and over 140 per cent respectively, will they feel any real improvement in their income situation.

The same applies when we want to tackle the poverty trap: we need more incentives for people to accept a job. In any case we will have to see to it that people who accept a job do not lose out financially. But it is of equal importance that benefit claimants cannot at will decline jobs that are offered to them in the framework of the comprehensive approach. In those cases, sanctions will have to be taken. For work always offers more perspectives, a life that is socially rich and meaningful, than a solitary and dreary existence on welfare.

We have to deal with a number of cumbersome obstacles in the Netherlands. We will have to clear these away if we want to avoid the pressure on social security becoming too great.

It is of the utmost importance that we keep a sharp eye on our surroundings, across the frontiers of our own nations and across the frontiers of the EU. In Europe we can still learn much from others without having to throw the achievements of the welfare state overboard, because it must be possible, somewhere between the US and Europe, to let the ship steer a middle course. But when we are talking about social policy there is one thing about which there is no doubt in my mind. Social policy starts with employment and ends with employment. That is the best guarantee for the future of the welfare state both in the Netherlands and in Europe.

Let me end by quoting Edmund Burke: a state without the means of some change is without the means of conservation. We have the means, so let's use them to the benefit of our future.

Welfare Reform: Germany

Wilfried Prewo

Finally, at long last, Germany is embarking on a debate on welfare reform. To be sure, the country is not embarking on a no-holds-barred overhaul of its social policies. Germany's political class is not ready to ditch the Bismarckian legacy of a paternalistic welfare state.

Nonetheless, the beginning of a welfare debate could mark a significant turning point in a country where any cuts in entitlements have previously been taboo and any such proposal was deemed utterly naïve, since it would be politically suicidal.

The debate is also telling, both in regard to policy—the theoretically best solution to a problem—and politics—when and how and in what variant, pure or watered down, political action is taken so as to curry the most favour with voters and to minimise backlash.

With over four million people unemployed, or close to ten per cent of the labour force, and another 2.68 million on welfare,[1] or about 3.3 per cent of the population of 82 million, and social transfers at about one third of GDP, the country might, indeed, consider giving itself a push to deregulate its labour market and reform its entitlement programmes.

German payroll taxes for health (14 per cent), pensions (over 19 per cent), and unemployment (6.5 per cent) have

---

Presentation at the Stockholm Network Conference on 'Europe's Welfare Burden – The Case for Reform', 1 February 2002, the Hague, Netherlands. This is an expanded and updated version of an op-ed piece which appeared in the *Wall Street Journal Europe*, 10 September 2001.

been on a continuous rise, as fewer workers have to support more entitlement recipients; the 40 per cent total of payroll taxes makes German jobs too expensive, powering a vicious cycle of new job losses; and the budgets of states and communities are bursting at the seams, since they have to pay for welfare benefits according to federally prescribed guidelines.

Such a system is not sustainable. Innovation-induced productivity gains could, for a while, keep Germany's products competitive in world markets, but globalisation has exposed the Achilles' heel of the welfare state. In a rash of countries, from Eastern Europe to South East Asia, the establishment of the rule of law and market-oriented reforms has given their producers access to mobile capital, while open world markets allow them to sell products of equal quality but at a far lower price, as they are not burdened with onerous social and labour laws.

> *'globalisation has exposed the Achilles' heel of the welfare state'*

This system is also unjust: supplementing welfare benefits with occasional black-market jobs as a painter or waitress, a person on welfare looks far more clever than his or her hard-working and tax-paying neighbour. Combining the welfare benefit with black-market income is a widespread abuse and is invited by the system's strong poison pill against regular jobs: apart from a minor deductible of about €140 per month, any income earned (and declared) will lead to an equal deduction in the welfare benefit, implying a marginal tax of 100 per cent. Furthermore, benefits are at a level where, depending on family size, a regular full-time job would have to pay a gross hourly wage of €6.50 for a single wage-earner without dependents, €7.50 for a single parent with one child, or €12 for a married person with two children to be worth more than welfare.[2] Apart from the fact that many welfare recipients are unskilled and cannot command an hourly wage of €10, in reality they would have to be offered a far higher wage, since it would have to exceed the sum of welfare benefit and black-market income. In the face of these disincentives which keep people locked in welfare, the average time spent on welfare has risen from about 25 months in 1997 to 31 months in 2000.

Of the 2.68 million recipients, about 0.9 million are considered to be able to work—after netting out welfare recipients over age 65 and under 15 and others with characteristics that prevent them (disability) or excuse them (small children) from work. About 1.2 million long-term unemployed[3] should be added to this figure, which would then yield a total of 2.1 million recipients who are capable of work. Any policy directed at them must address two issues: make work, not aid, the only option and make work pay, i.e. turn the monetary disincentive against regular work into an incentive by reducing the currently prohibitive marginal tax.

In the United States, the monetary disincentive to taking a job is being overcome by the earned income tax credit, a variant of the negative income tax. In Germany, owing to institutional and other characteristics, different concepts, though related in spirit, are being debated under the term *Kombilohn* or 'combination wage': by combining wage and aid, the concept of the *Kombilohn* was meant to mitigate the prohibitive marginal tax of 100 per cent which would otherwise be levied on any wage income of a welfare recipient. Similar to a negative income tax, the level of aid would decrease as wage income rises and would eventually be phased out. The debate on the *Kombilohn* is still at an early stage in Germany. A federal and universal *Kombilohn*-model does not yet exist, since, so far, the labour unions have been successful in opposing it (for fear of increasing downward pressure on the lower end of the wage scale). However, with unemployment over four million, the Schroeder government in January 2002 declared its intention to install a federal *Kombilohn* programme.[4] It remains to be seen whether that will become law in the face of union opposition and the upcoming election in Autumn 2002.

The core issue of any welfare reform, however, is making work, not aid, the only option for welfare recipients who are capable of working. So far, it has been taboo to deny aid to people that were not willing to work. Worse, many politicians have steadfastly denied that such abuse of the social system exists. Any proposal to strip people of benefits if they declined a job offer was considered cold-hearted. But the political climate has gradually changed.

First, claims of abuse can no longer be denied or belittled as exceptional cases in an otherwise worthy and well-functioning system. Many German households turn to black-market help for anything from cleaning and gardening to house and auto repairs, as they cannot get their demands met in the regular economy. Compared with the OECD average, Germany shows an employment gap of close to one million jobs requiring lower or no skills;[5] and half of the officially registered job openings are in this category, indicating that the number of jobs available in the lower skill categories roughly matches the number of those that are capable of working. Some welfare agencies which have called in recipients and offered them jobs found that, miraculously, the recipients disappeared. A Dutch welfare organisation, Maatwerk, which had received a contract from the City of Hannover to place welfare recipients into jobs, had this experience: about one third of the recipients responded that they did not need Maatwerk's services; they were puzzled that a welfare agency wanted to place them into a job, claiming that this is none of the agency's business, it should just hand them a cheque and then leave them alone; some even openly admitted that they already had a job (in the black market), a response which should have triggered an immediate end to welfare were it not for the combined efforts of publicly paid lawyers who declared all of this a misunderstanding and the well-meaning nature of the social workers who did not want their rolls diminished.

Second, the cost of welfare is driving communities towards insolvency and forcing them to cut back on other expenditures, from schools to infrastructure. Citizens view

> 'Citizens view welfare no longer as a burden which they have to accept in the name of solidarity, but as utterly wasteful'

welfare no longer as a burden which they have to accept in the name of solidarity, but as utterly wasteful. They complain about the trade-offs in reduced and essential public services. Combined with widely publicised cases of abuse, the pressure on politicians has been rising.

The political Left has been unable to put forth a reform proposal. First, it counted on the welfare recipients as its constituents, although that may be a false hope, since many of them do not vote. But certainly the 'poverty industry' is a major Social Democratic constituency. First, there are the welfare bureaucrats whose jobs, status and agency size depend on the number of recipients on their rolls; diminishing the number on welfare rolls diminishes the bureaucracy's role. Second, there are the non-profit organisations, church-linked or not, that contract with the welfare agencies and depend on public money. Third, there are social welfare lawyers who see to it that the recipients get what they feel entitled to (such cases in Germany may deal with the question of whether a twelve-year-old should receive, from the government a new rather than a used bicycle). And, finally, the social policy legislators who pride themselves on providing all that, albeit with other people's money.

One would have thought that the political Right would have viewed this as a unique opportunity to advance its own proposals. However, while the German Christian Democratic Union (CDU), being the more or less conservative party, is not, to the same degree as the Social Democrats, the hostage of the poverty industry, it has, in the past, also shied away from welfare reform. The party had always bloodied its nose when proposing reform. Each time it tried, the Social Democrats could put the antisocial label on the CDU, accusing it of trying to axe the welfare state and charging that CDU proposals came from a cold heart, lacking any empathy. And, although welfare recipients were not an important group at the voting booth, the Social Democrats could portray CDU proposals as a harbinger for equally cruel measures to be expected by pensioners and others. The CDU could not, by itself, design a policy which would reconcile the need to reform welfare with the imperative to be compassionate to the poor. Luckily, help came from overseas.

By 1998, word from Wisconsin's welfare reform, or more aptly, *welfare replacement*, had spread to Germany. The Hudson Institute, itself involved in Wisconsin, was instrumental in acquainting European policy makers and think tanks with 'Wisconsin Works'. As the success of Wisconsin's policy became evident and indisputable, these voices found more listeners in the CDU. Finally, the prime minister of the state of Hesse, Roland Koch, put forth a proposal which, down to many details, is a carbon copy of Wisconsin Works. Its main ingredients are:

- Priority for work, not aid: the beneficiary is entitled to help in finding a job or in job-training; benefits are tied to a recipient's taking a job or undergoing training.

- Restructuring of job placement and aid agencies: the two tasks and the respective monies are merged in job centres which will have sole responsibility for placing long-term unemployed and welfare recipients. Private and non-profit agencies may also bid to be designated as job centres.

- Binding agreement (*Hesse-Pact*) between individual job seeker and job centre on respective rights and duties; the recipient must himself make an effort to find a job.

- Stricter requirements and expectations: a recipient must accept a job which pays less than current benefits; combination with subsidies such as provided by the *Kombilohn*-concept; welfare recipients must register themselves as job-seekers.

- Sanctions for non-compliance: aid can be denied if the recipient does not fulfil his side of the bargain.

- Reward for success: successful job centres receive monetary incentives.

- Promoting the low-wage sector: by making use of the *Kombilohn*-concept, low-wage jobs in the private sector are promoted as an alternative to public works jobs or community service projects.

- Systemic competition and federal waiver: the individual federal states may opt for their individual programmes; states can shape job placement programmes at the state level.

Simply put, the proposal by Hesse makes job placement rather than handing out a welfare cheque the number one priority. To this end, it seeks to merge the job placement functions of the (federal) labour offices with the communities' welfare agencies into job centres. Needless to say, this also implies a partial transfer of the labour agencies' job placement funds to the new job centres. Similar to the US federal welfare reform of 1996, the partial transfer of federal authority and money to the states and communities requires federal legislation which Hesse submitted in January 2002.[6] It resembles the US legislation in that it gives the states a waiver from current federal programmes and allows them to experiment with a new approach. No state would be forced to follow Hesse's chosen path of emulating Wisconsin. (This aspect will also be interesting for the German federalism debate.)

> *'The Hesse proposal of replacing the welfare handout with a helping hand in finding a job is not just good policy, but good politics'*

The Hesse proposal of replacing the welfare handout with a helping hand in finding a job is not just good policy, but good politics as well. With the Wisconsin model, the CDU, finally, has an effective, compassionate proposal. Nobody can criticise it for trying to scrimp welfare recipients for money, as a Wisconsin-type reform will, initially, cost more money. The party can claim that it cares for welfare recipients, that it wants to put them back on their feet, not just hand them a cheque and send them off.

For many years, German conservatives have thought that market-oriented social policy reform is necessary but best avoided, since as a party, the CDU always lost votes with market-oriented reforms. If the party realises that it will succeed if it proposes market-oriented reforms that are compassionate as well, this will have significance for upcoming debates on social policy, most prominently for health and pension reform.

Welfare Reform: Sweden

Benny Carlson

Sweden is not well known for its innovations in welfare reform—far from it. However, it is possible to make some comparisons between developments in the welfare area—interpreted in its more narrow American sense (means-tested cash benefits)—in the United States and Sweden, first at a macro and then at a micro level.

Unemployment is generally regarded as the main structural factor behind variations in the number of people on welfare.[1] A comparison of unemployment in the United States and Sweden during the 1990s (Figure 1, p. 49) makes it obvious that the conditions for developments in the welfare area have been quite different in the two countries.

The United States had steady economic growth and falling unemployment from 1992 and onwards. Sweden had a severe economic crisis in the early 1990s and unemployment went up from 1.7 per cent in 1990 to 9.1 per cent in 1993 (OECD figures). At the same time there was a great influx of refugees from the former Yugoslavia.

Not surprisingly, welfare caseloads in the two countries look quite different. In the American case, most recipients (under Aid to Families with Dependent Children and after welfare reform under Temporary Assistance for Needy Families) are single mothers, while in Sweden most recipients of cash benefits are people without children. As a matter of fact, single men without children make up about one-third of the caseload.

In the United States, welfare reform was launched in 1996, in the midst of a decade-long period of economic growth and caseloads fell sharply—by more than 50 per cent between 1996 and 2000—as can be seen from Fig. 2 (p. 50).

48

49

Figure 1: Standardised Unemployment in US and Sweden, 1990 - 2000

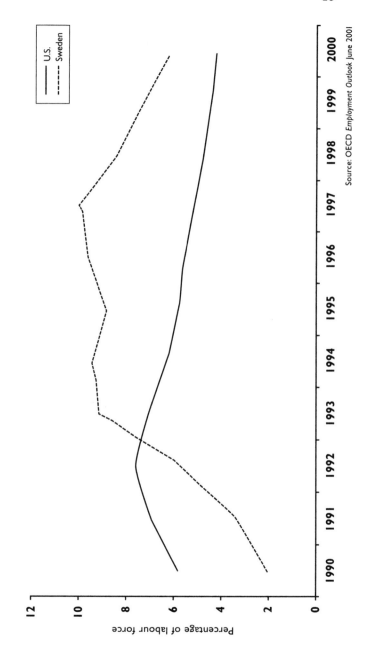

Source: OECD *Employment Outlook* June 2001

Figure 2: Welfare Caseloads in US and Sweden, 1990 - 2000

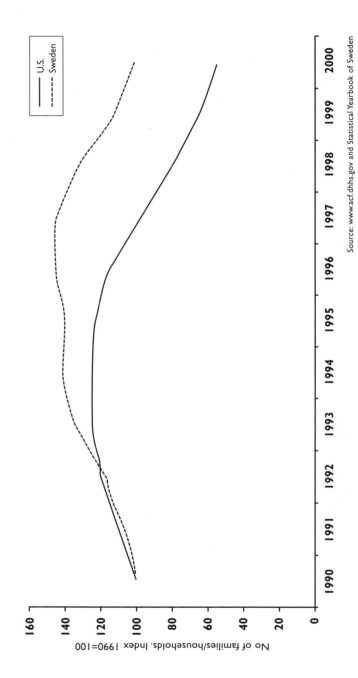

Source: www.acf.dhhs.gov and Statistical Yearbook of Sweden

In Sweden the caseload followed the unemployment pattern closely and did not begin to decline until 1998. Swedish development has been even more gloomy than these caseload figures suggest. The time people spent on welfare increased and total costs more than doubled between 1990 and 1997.

The US caseload amounted to about five per cent of the population in 1990 and two per cent in 2000; the Swedish caseload came to about six per cent of the population in 1990 and remained the same a decade later in 2000.

Consequently, economic conditions and caseloads in the United States and Sweden developed quite differently during the 1990s. What about the organisation of the Swedish welfare system compared to the American?

In the United States welfare reform was a devolution revolution, in other words, responsibility for the welfare system devolved from federal government to the states, who receive federal money (block grants) provided that they comply with certain rules and reach certain results. In Sweden responsibility for and financing of welfare has always rested with the municipalities at the same time as the government attempts to set standards. There is a law regulating welfare. There are courts creating precedents. There is a National Board of Health and Welfare interpreting the law and court decisions. The law states that anyone qualified for welfare should receive assistance that guarantees 'a reasonable standard of living' and the National Board tries to decide what this really means.

Most discussions in the 1990s have concerned this welfare norm, *not* welfare reform. The result was a norm supposed to guarantee a basic uniformity in the country *and* freedom for municipalities to decide for themselves what benefits they want to supply above the norm. There are, as a result of this, quite big differences in benefits between different municipalities.

The general trend during the 1990s was that the municipalities became more restrictive to keep costs down. One main aspect of these restrictions is that people have to take part in work-like activities and job-search to a higher degree.

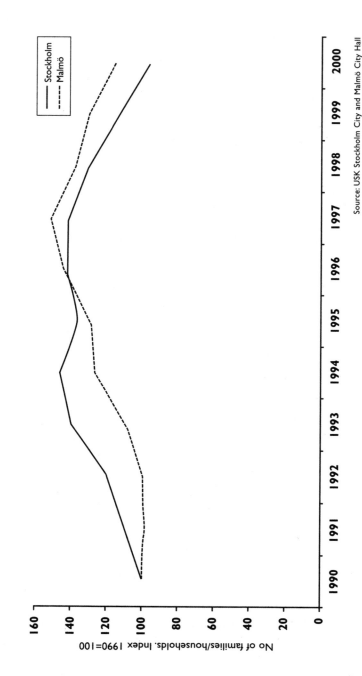

Figure 3: Welfare Caseloads in Stockholm and Malmö, 1990 - 2000

Source: USK Stockholm City and Malmö City Hall

Some municipalities have been inspired by a Danish experiment, the Farum model, which has some resemblance to the American model. Under the Farum model, the municipalities themselves act as labour exchanges— sometimes relying on community service jobs—and threaten to cut people off from welfare immediately if they do not accept a job offer.

Stockholm and Malmö are Sweden's biggest and third biggest municipalities or cities. From Figure 3 (p. 52) we can conclude that the welfare caseloads in these cities show the same pattern as could be observed at the national level, although things happen a bit later in Malmö.

In Stockholm the number of people on welfare was reduced by 35 per cent from 1997 to 2000 and costs were reduced by 28 per cent. These results are said to be due primarily to increased cooperation with employers and temping agencies. The present aim is very ambitious: to reduce the number of people on welfare by 50 per cent from 1999 to 2004.

If one wants to know something about what is going on when it comes to moving people from welfare to work, which is the essence of welfare reform, one has to get down to the micro level in both the United States and Sweden, since experiments in both countries are carried out at the local level. A short comparison between a typical job centre in Detroit, Michigan, and a new type of job centre in Malmö (partially funded with government money), based on first-hand knowledge (observation and interviews) provides some interesting insights.

The social welfare authority (Family Independence Agency, FIA) in Michigan is, to quote Carol Weissert,[2] by tradition 'hierarchical, rule-bound, and state-dominated'. The labour market programmes under the Michigan Department of Career Development (MDCD), on the other hand, are decentralised, with local Workforce Development Boards as the main actors. In Sweden, it has more or less been the other way around. The social welfare system is decentralised and the labour exchanges are rather hierarchical and rule-bound.

Table 1
Comparisons Between Job Centres in Detroit and Malmö

	Detroit	Malmö
Co-operation between authorities	Strong	Strong
Co-operation with employers	Strong	Weak so far
Use of incentives	Strong	Weak
Problems with child and health care	Big	Small
Career centres	Often	No
Private contractors	Yes	No
Work first	Yes	More so lately
Job retention	Important	Under-developed

In Michigan and Detroit, social welfare agencies and job centres have been working closely together on welfare reform, although their staffs do not live close by to one another. In Malmö, new job centres were created in 1999. Here representatives from the municipality, the labour exchange and the social security agency work closely together in the same localities in order to come to grips with people's problems instead of shuffling people back and forth between different authorities.

In Michigan and Detroit, employers have a decisive influence over job centres. They constitute the majority in Workforce Development Boards and they are very visible at job centres, interviewing job applicants. In Malmö, co-operation with employers has so far been quite weak. They are not represented on the board and not visible at job centres. But there is at least an awareness that increased cooperation with employers is desirable.

American welfare reform makes use of several sticks and carrots. Michigan is less keen on using sticks than most other states, having no five-year lifetime limit for people on welfare. In Sweden and Malmö there is not much talk—at least not officially—about incentives.

In America, child and health care are major obstacles on the road from welfare to work. In Sweden, these problems are small. The only potential problem is that it may take some time to get a child into a childcare centre.

In Michigan and Detroit, many job centres have—in line with intentions in the Workforce Investment Act of 1998—developed into career centres. In Sweden, you could say that the traditional labour exchanges are indeed career centres—trying to help everybody to get a job or a better job. However, they have not been able to solve the complex problems of immigrants, and therefore in areas with many immigrants new job centres have been instituted.

In Detroit, different private for-profit, non-profit and public contractors work together in job centres. In Malmö all employees at a job centre are from the public sector.

American welfare reform has, as is well known, at least up to the 2001 recession, been leaning towards 'work first'. In Malmö, there have been different opinions on this. The group targeted at the new job centres is supposed to be 'one year from the labour market'. Some case managers consequently say that you have to work with these people for a year or so to get them ready for market entry. Others admit they can never tell when someone is ready for job-search and that you therefore should put them to the test as soon as possible.

Job centres in Detroit emphasise the importance of job retention, to avoid having former welfare recipients returning to welfare. In Malmö, efforts to follow up former programme participants at their present work places have so far not been very developed, but will probably be given more priority in the future.

So, although there has been no welfare reform from above in Sweden, there are some winds of change blowing from below (with the help of money from above), and there are, as this tentative 'micro comparison' has demonstrated, differences as well as similarities between what is going on in Sweden and the United States. For now, though, Sweden still has a long way to go if it wants to achieve anything like the reduction in caseloads that the US has seen in recent years.

Notes

Jason A. Turner

1   In particular, the House legislation would require:

- Seventy per cent of each state's welfare adult population be participating in welfare-to-work activities by 2007, if they are not working in the private economy.

- For the state to count an adult as participating, he or she must be attending a work activity on a full-time basis, defined as 40 hours per week. Furthermore, at least 24 of the 40 hours must be in actual work activity such as helping out in a government office, working for a non-profit organisation, or perhaps working in an outdoor setting. The other 16 hours can be in work or any other constructive activity, such as training, education or substance abuse treatment.

- After the second month of non-participation, a state is not permitted to make any benefit payment to the family until the adult returns to his or her assignment (in a provision which needs to be fixed, this requirement applies everywhere except in the two largest states, California and New York).

- States can test new ideas using a 'superwaiver authority' which allows the Governor to apply to the federal government to combine welfare, food stamps, public housing and various training programmes into one comprehensive work programme. Under this provision states could, for instance, design universal work requirements for means-tested benefits of all kinds. Individuals seeking low-cost public housing would be required to work in exchange for the subsidy, just as they now must work for welfare benefits.

  The net result of this superwaiver authority may be to encourage state governors to produce the next generation of ideas and solutions to the problem of expanding government and its corresponding tendency to create and increase family dependency.

Alan Deacon

1 Wilson, J.Q., *On Character*, Washington DC: The AEI Press, 1995, p. 206. The ways in which conflicting perspectives on welfare are grounded in different understandings of human nature is explored in Deacon, A., *Perspectives on Welfare: Ideas, Ideologies and Policy Debates*, Buckingham: Open University Press, 2002.

2 The best source for Titmuss's writings is the recently published collection, Alcock, P., Glennerster, H., Oakley, A. and Sinfield, A. (eds), *Welfare and Well-being: Titmuss's Contribution to Social Policy*, Bristol: Policy Press, 2001.

3 Titmuss, R.M., *Commitment to Welfare*, Unwin University Books, 1968, p. 69.

4 Titmuss, R.M., *Parents Revolt*, London: Secker and Warburg, 1942, p. 120. For an interesting discussion of Titmuss's view on problem families see Welshman, J., 'Evacuation, hygiene, and social policy: the Our Towns report of 1943', *The Historical Journal*, 42, 3, 1999, pp. 781-807.

5 Titmuss, R.M., *The Gift Relationship*, London: George Allen and Unwin, 1970, p. 239.

6 Titmuss, *The Gift Relationship*, p. 239.

7 The quotations that follow are taken from Murray's first book, *Losing Ground*, New York: Basic Books, 1984. For the subsequent changes in Murray's position, especially in relation to the importance of out-of-wedlock births, see: Murray, C., 'The coming white underclass', *Wall St Journal*, October 29, 1993; 'Charles Murray' in Nye, R. (ed.), *The Future of Welfare*, London: Social Market Foundation, 1998; *Underclass + 10: Charles Murray and the British Underclass 1990-2000*, London: Civitas, 2001.

8 Teles, S., *Whose Welfare? AFDC and Elite Politics*, University of Kansas Press, 1996, p. 157.

9 *Losing Ground*.

10 *Losing Ground*, p. 155.

11 The best sources for the development of Field's thinking are; Field, F., *Making Welfare Work*, London: Institute of Community Studies, 1995; 'A rejoinder' in Deacon, A. (ed.), *Stakeholder Welfare*, London: IEA, 1996; *Reforming Welfare*, London: Social Market Foundation, 1997; *Reflections on Welfare Reform*, London: Social Market Foundation, 1998.

12 Field, *Reforming Welfare*, p. 26.

13 The best sources for Mead's ideas are; *Beyond Entitlement*, New York: Free Press, 1986; 'The hidden jobs debate', *Public Interest*, 91, 1988, pp. 40-58; *The New Politics of Poverty*, New York: Basic Books, 1992; *The New Paternalism*, Washington DC: Brookings Institution Press, 1997.

14 Mead, L.M., 'The Rise of Paternalism, in Mead, L.M. (ed.), *The New Paternalism: Supervisory Approaches to Poverty*, Washington DC, Brookings Institution Press, 1997, pp. 27-28.

15 These quotations are taken from the 'Responsive Communitarian Platform', in Etzioni, A. (ed.), *The Essential Communitarian Reader*, Oxford: Rowan and Littlefield, 1998. The discussion of Etzioni's thinking draws primarily upon *The New Golden Rule*, London: Profile Books, 1997.

16 Sacks, J., *The Politics of Hope*, London: Jonathan Cape, 1997.

17 This claim is made, for example, in Blair, T., *The Third Way: New Politics for the New Century*, London: Fabian Society, 1998.

Wilfried Prewo

1 In the year 2000.

2 Institut der Deutschen Wirtschaft, Cologne, Stellungnahme zur Öffentlichen Anhörung des Ausschusses für Arbeit und Sozialordnung des Deutschen Bundestages (Statement at the Public Hearing of the Bundestag Labor and Social Policy Committee), 28 January 28 2002, p. 6.

3 Germany has a generous and two-tiered unemployment benefit system. Unemployment insurance (*Arbeitslosengeld*) provides coverage for 6 to 12 months

for those under 45, the length depending on prior employment. Those above 45 can be covered for as much as 32 months. The benefits of an unemployed person with at least one child amount to 67 per cent, for others 60 per cent, of the net wage. Those still unemployed after the coverage period receive reduced aid of 57 and 53 per cent respectively (*Arbeitslosenhilfe*); this benefit is also handled by the labour office (*Arbeitsamt*) and is thus a federal programme. It is supposed to be limited to one extra year, but can be renewed indefinitely and depends on the beneficiary's ability and willingness to work. When beneficiaries fail that test, they become recipients of welfare (*Sozialhilfe*), which is administered and paid for by communities and the federal states (*Laender*) according to federal guidelines (*Bundessozialhilfegesetz*).

4   The current Kombilohn experiments in the states of Rheinland-Pfalz or Saarland do not chiefly address the marginal tax hurdle. The Rheinland-Pfalz model chiefly attempts to reduce the financial burden on communities; furthermore, it tends to steer people into part-time rather than full-time jobs. Other concepts, such as the proposal of the German Federation of Employers' Associations, are closer in spirit to the EITC by suggesting that 25 per cent of wage income should not be offset by a reduction in welfare benefits; this, in effect, would reduce the marginal tax from 100 to 75 per cent.

5   Institut der Deutschen Wirtschaft, *op. cit.*, p. 3.

6   Entwurf eines Gesetzes zum optimalen Fördern und Fordern in Vermittlungsagenturen (OFFENSIV-Gesetz), Gesetzesantrag des Landes Hessen, and accompanying press releases, Wiesbaden, 24 January 2002.

Benny Carlson

1   A considerable proportion of welfare recipients in Sweden—especially in the big cities—are immigrants and young people. Here employment would be a better structural factor to look out for, since many immigrants and youngsters have never even 'advanced' to the category of unemployed. Between 1990-91 and 1998-99 employment in the whole Swedish population fell eight

percentage points from 81 to 73 per cent. Among the foreign-born, employment fell 15 percentage points from 70 to 55 per cent and, among 16 to 29-year-olds, 16 percentage points from 68 to 52 per cent. See *Välfärdsbokslut för 1990-talet. Slutbetänkande från Kommittén Välfärdsbokslut* (SOU 2001:79) pp. 37, 78.

2   Weissert, C., 'Michigan's Welfare Reform: Generous But Tough', in Weissert, C. (ed.), *Learning From Leaders: Welfare Reform, Politics and Policy in Five Midwestern States*, Albany NY: Rockefeller Institute Press, 2000, p. 157.